EDITOR: LEE JOHNSON

OSPREY
MILITARY

NEW VANGUARD

10

WARRIOR
MECHANISED COMBAT
VEHICLE 1987-1994

Text by
CHRIS FOSS
Colour plates by
PETER SARSON

First published in Great Britain in 1994 by Osprey, an imprint of Reed Consumer Books Limited, Michelin House, 81 Fulham Road, London SW3 6RB and Auckland, Melbourne, Singapore and Toronto.

ISBN 1 85532 379 6
Filmset in Great Britain
Printed through Bookbuilders Ltd, Hong Kong

Acknowledgements
I should like to extend my thanks to a number of people without whose help and advice this book would not have been possible: Will Fowler, Simon Dunstan, Major Len Brown ITDU Warminster, Major John Rochelle MC STAFFORDS, Major Tim Sandiford STAFFORDS.

Editor's Note
Readers may wish to read this title in conjunction with the following Osprey titles:
Desert Storm Special 1 *Land Power*
Elite 46 *Armies of the Gulf War*

For a catalogue of all books published by Osprey Military please write to:

**The Marketing Manager,
Consumer Catalogue Department,
Osprey Publishing Ltd,
Michelin House, 81 Fulham Road,
London Sw3 6RB**

WARRIOR MCV-80

DESIGN AND DEVELOPMENT

Armoured personnel carriers (APCs) did not enter service with the British Army in significant numbers until the early fifties. During the Second World War a large number of Bren Gun Carriers were used to give infantry on the move some armoured protection, but it was not until 1943 that the benefit of delivering protected troops to the forward line of battle was acted upon. Even then all that was available were converted vehicles such as the Kangaroo, a turretless Sherman or Ram tank with infantry riding in the fighting compartment, or American M3 half-tracks.

Early APCs

A radical re-think of the role of mechanised infantry after the war resulted in the development of the FV603 Alvis Saracen (6x6) vehicle. The prototype was completed in 1952 (a process accelerated by the Malayan Emergency) with the first production vehicles becoming available the follow-

ing year. A member of the FV600 series of fighting vehicles, which also included the FV601 Saladin (6x6) armoured car armed with a 76mm gun, a total of 1,838 were built for the home and export markets with final deliveries being made in 1972. The Saracen was not finally phased out of British Army service until 1993 when a small unit in Hong Kong was disbanded. In addition to the Alvis Saracen APC, the British Army deployed significant numbers of FV1611 Humber one-ton (4x4) APCs together with a number of specialised variants including radio, command vehicle and anti-tank with Malkara anti-tank guided weapons (ATGWs).

One of the prototypes of the GKN Defence Warrior. The vehicle has extra track links on the forward hull and hessian scrim is in position to cover the headlights to cut out reflection, and along the sides of the vehicles, to be lowered to cover the shadow around the wheels and tracks when the vehicle is static and under a camouflage net. The four blocks mounted just to the left of the gun mantlet are the Royal Ordnance VIRSS (Visual and Infra-Red Smoke Screening System) which was not adopted for production vehicles. The dischargers on the other side are just visible The infantry wear '58 pattern webbing and are armed with the L1A1 7.62mm SLR.

One of the original GKN Defence Warriors with driver's hatch open and showing two lifting points on *either side of the hull and without skirts which were fitted to production vehicles.*

The FV432 series

In the late 1950s the then GKN Fighting Vehicle Development Division (FVDD) was awarded a contract by the Ministry of Defence for the construction of four prototypes and ten trials vehicles of the FV420 unarmoured tracked vehicle and these were all delivered by 1958. GKN FVDD was then awarded a contract for the design and development of the FV430 series of armoured fighting vehicles (AFV) with the initial contract covering the supply of four prototype vehicles and a further 13 for troop trials. In conjunction with this move the then Royal Ordnance Factories were awarded a contract to build a further seven troop trial vehicles under GKN's design parentage.

GKN FVDD and the Royal Ordnance Factories completed all of these vehicles by 1961 and the following year the company, which is today is known as GKN Defence, was awarded its first production contract for the FV432 APC, the first production vehicles being completed in 1963. Using the same basic chassis, GKN was also awarded a contract to design and build the FV431 Light Tracked Load Carrier and the FV434 Fitters Vehicle. The latter subsequently entered production, but the FV431 was not developed past the prototype stage.

Production of the FV432 was undertaken by GKN at Telford in Shropshire and some 3000 FV432 series APCs were built for the British Army before production was completed in 1971. The only export customer was India, which purchased a few FV432 command vehicles for use with its Abbot 105mm self-propelled guns. The FV433 Abbot 105mm self-propelled gun was developed by Vickers Defence Systems and uses automotive components of the FV432 series of APCs including powerpack and suspension.

Although the GKN Defence Warrior is now replacing the FV432 in many roles, the British Army still had over 1000 vehicles in service in 1993. Many specialised versions of the FV432

used by the mechanised infantry battalions of the British Army will continue into service well into the future, for example the 81mm self-propelled mortar. The FV432 fulfils much the same role in the British Army as the very similiar United States FMC M113 series of full tracked APCs, but the FV432, as does the M113, lacks the armour, mobility and firepower to operate with the latest MBTs as part of the combined arms team.

Project Definition 1
The initial proposals to consider future APC requirements for the British Army were undertaken between 1969 and 1971 by the then Fighting Vehicles Research and Development Establishment at Chertsey (this subsequently became the Military Vehicles and Engineering Establishment and is today part of the Defence Research Agency). The original concept was for a much heavier vehicle weighing around 30 tons, powered by a 750 hp diesel engine, a turret armed with a 30mm Rarden cannon and fitted with

One of the Warrior prototypes showing the overall layout of the vehicle with turret in the centre and troop compartment at the rear. Note roof plate with adjacent infantry observation periscopes and rear roof hatches. This also has early model stowage bins attached to the rear of the vehicle, but lacks any other external stowage. The design of the vehicle with the engine to the front not only allows easy exit from the rear, but gives added protection from any frontal shots that may impact on the vehicle.

Chobham armour to give a high degree of battlefield survivability, but this was abandoned for cost reasons. An automotive test rig was built at Chertsey.

First industrial involvement came in 1972 when all United Kingdom manufacturers were invited to offer themselves as potential main contractors for PD1 (Project Definition 1) studies. As a result GKN and Vickers Defence Systems were selected to undertake competitive studies. Following completion of PD1 the firms were involved in a tendering exercise as one part of the 1972-1976 studies.

Then in 1976, as the programme became more

The first Warrior prototypes had twin doors in the rear of the hull as here, but these proved to be difficult to open in some tactical situations so production vehicles have a single power-operated door in the rear, although the roof hatches were retained. The turret periscopes are clearly visible, and just to the left of the commander can be seen the split mirror traversable periscope. (Terry J. Gander)

clearly defined, the MoD decided for the first time in an armoured vehicle programme that full responsibility for the development project should be vested in a prime contractor and, following competitive tendering between GKN and Vickers, the former was appointed.

Mechanised Combat Vehicle-80

Full project definition was undertaken from 1977 to 1979 by the then GKN Sankey after its competitive selection as prime contractor for the MCV-80 (Mechanised Combat Vehicle-80), as it was subsequently called. At that time the US was also developing a new infantry fighting vehicle. Accordingly between 1978 and 1980 a parallel evaluation of the FMC XM2 (subsequently type classified as the M2 Bradley) took place. In 1979 full development started of the MCV-80, although studies of the XM2 continued.

In June 1980 the MoD selected MCV-80 to meet the requirements of the British Army; by that time three prototypes of the MCV-80 had already been completed. The first of these was the suspension test rig followed by two mobile test rigs, one of which had the two-man turret armed with a 30mm Rarden cannon and one with a turret mounted 7.62mm machine gun (MG).

MCV-80 was designed to meet General Staff Requirement 3533 for a vehicle with:
a. Capacity for 10 men including driver and gunner together with their combat supplies.

b. Sufficient mobility to allow it to keep tactical station with the Challenger 1 MBT.
c. Protection against specified indirect artillery shell bursts and direct small arms/MG fire.
d. Firepower in anti-light armour, general support and some air defence roles.

GKN Defence was the first company in the UK to run Prime Contractorship for an AFV; in 1979 they were selected to prime the Warrior development programme. Development of the Warrior was carried out to time and cost under target incentive contract conditions. As prime contractor GKN Defence had full responsibility for the product and programme, enabling the company to meet the delivery schedules for production deliveries to the British Army. If the production and performance targets had not been met strict contract penalty conditions would have been triggered.

The British Army required a high degree of reliability in the Warrior family and this was achieved in the development programme, 12 prototype vehicles and test rigs clocking up over 200,000 km plus extensive ballistic tests. During the 1991 Gulf Campaign, some 300 Warriors in all configurations were deployed and travelled some 330,000 km in desert conditions and had a demonstrated reliability level of 95 per cent.

Integration of design, development and production enabled GKN to maximise the benefits of concurrent engineering as production engineering

requirements were taken into account in the design and development phases. During the Warrior programme some 9000 drawings, 250 components and sub-systems and vehicle specifications and process specifications were produced and components sourced from 600 suppliers.

By being selected as the prime contractor, GKN Defence could select hardware which gave the best value and components and sub-systems were no longer specified as 'free issue' by the MoD. GKN invited competitive tenders for many of the sub-systems. For example the Royal Ordnance 30mm Rarden cannon was subsequently manufactured by the British Manufacture and Research Company. Pilkington PE were the original developer and supplier of the Raven sights for the commander and gunner, but Avimo was also awarded a significant contract as a result of competitive tendering. This aimed to drive costs down and provide better value for money.

Compared with the earlier FV432, the Warrior is a much more complicated vehicle and many of the specialised variants have a high level of systems integration. In 1984 the MoD announced that negotiations were taking place with GKN for the initial production batch of MCV-80 vehicles

Warrior mechanised combat vehicle operating with a Vickers Defence Systems Challenger 1 MBT during early trials in Germany. Note the side skirts and additional stowage facilities not present on the prototype. In addition the original double doors at the rear of the troop compartment have now been replaced by the single door. The Warrior has camouflage net stowed in the open bins along the top of the hull. This camouflage net can be quickly deployed if the vehicle is static or in a hide.

but that future orders would be open to competitive tendering by GKN and other qualified manufacturers. A total of 12 Warrior prototypes were built, four of these being used in 'Exercise Lionheart' in Germany in the autumn of 1984 when Warrior demonstrated that it could operate with the Challenger 1 MBT. In November 1984 the MCV-80 was accepted for service with the British Army, this being the date laid down at the tender stage of the programme in 1976; the vehicle was named 'Warrior' the following year.

Warrior production
In addition to winning the initial production contract for the Warrior, in 1985 the MoD announced that at as result of competitive bidding the company would also be awarded the contract for the

The complete powerpack of the Warrior consisting of a Perkins Engines CV8 TCA V-8 diesel engine and a General Motors X-300-4B fully automatic transmission. This is supplied as a single unit by Perkins Engines ready for installation in the vehicle.

second and third production batches, the total British Army order comprising 1053 vehicles. The other contenders for the contract were Alvis, Royal Ordnance and Vickers Defence Systems. It is interesting to note that the original requirement was for some 1900 Warrior vehicles at a cost of around £1.2 billion, but as a result of the 1981 Defence Review (DPP81) measures this was cut to 602 vehicles with 30mm Rarden turrets and the remainder without the 30mm Rarden.

Production of the Warrior commenced at a new purpose built facility at Telford, Shropshire, in January 1986 with the first production vehicles being completed in December the same year. The first production batch comprised 290 vehicles of which 170 were section vehicles with the two-man turret and 30mm Rarden cannon, the remaining 120 being specialised variants.

The first production Warrior was formally handed over to the British Army in May 1987 at Telford, the 1st Battalion Grenadier Guards, part of the British Army of the Rhine (BAOR), being declared operational in mid-1988. The second unit to receive the Warrior was the 1st Battalion the Staffordshire Regiment (Prince of Wales) who

took delivery of their first vehicles in 1988. Additional details of the current Warrior battalion organisation are given in the chapter, Operational History.

While the Warrior is a considerable improvement over the earlier FV432 APC, many of the Warrior support vehicles are still FV432s or members of the Alvis Scorpion family of Combat Vehicle Reconnaissance (Tracked) which do not have the same degree of protection or battlefield manoeuvrability as the Warrior. For example, the 81mm mortars are still mounted in FV432s and originally the Milan ATGW teams were also carried in FV432s although as a result of the Gulf Conflict additional Warriors have been purchased for this role.

GKN build the complete hull of the Warrior section vehicle with Vickers Defence Systems supplying the two man turret ready for installation on the hull. Perkins Engines (Shrewsbury) provide the complete powerpack ready for installation in the vehicle. All of the specialised versions of Warrior are built by GKN.

As previously stated, the original British Army requirement was for a total of 1053 (later trimmed to 1048) Warrior vehicles – sufficient to equip a total of 13 mechanised infantry battalions plus vehicles for war reserve, maintenance float, training (including British Army Training Unit Suffield in Canada) and trials work. As a result of 'Options for Change' the size of the British Army is being dramatically reduced and the total requirement has now been reduced to 787 (including the three lost during Operation 'Desert Storm') with final deliveries due late in 1994.

Under 'Options for Change' the British Army will have a total of six armoured infantry battalions in Germany at part of the Allied Command Europe Rapid Reaction Corps (ARRC): two each with 4, 7 and 20 Armoured Brigades, and two in the UK, one with 1 Mechanised Brigade and one with 19 Mechanised Brigade.

Overseas Trials

At an early stage GKN started export marketing of the Warrior to a number of selected countries and by early 1993 the vehicle had been demonstrated or evaluated in a number of countries including France, Jordan, Kuwait, Norway, Oman, Saudi Arabia, Turkey and the United Arab Emirates.

This Pilkington PE Osprey combined day/night/thermal/laser sighting system is as fitted to the Warrior Mechanised Artillery Observation Vehicle (MAOV) used by the Royal Artillery. The Osprey system can be used as light-hot or dark-hot according to the optical conditions. This means that the heat from vehicles appears on the screen either as a light pattern or a dark pattern. This can be useful when visual conditions are marginal and the observer is trying to determine what he has seen on the screen. (Pilkington PE)

Table A: Warrior procurement		
Variant	Original Contract	Post Options
Section vehicle	595	387[1]
Trigat Medium Range	–	105[2]
Command vehicles	146	84
MCRV	110	103[3]
MRV(R)	67	39
Battery command vehicle	35	19
OPV	95	52
Total	1048	787

Notes:
1. Includes three section vehicles to replace those lost in 1991 conflict; total fleet will consist of 784 vehicles when deliveries are complete.
2. Medium Range Trigat was not part of original contract but was added in 1991. In the interim these are being used for the Milan ATGW teams.
3. An additional two vehicles have been approved since SDE bringing the total to 789.

Source: *House of Commons Session 1992-93, Defence Committee, First Report, Statement of the Defence Estimates 1992, 11th November 1992.*

INSIDE THE WARRIOR

The hull of Warrior is of all-welded aluminium armour construction which provides protection against small arms fire and shell splinters. Exact details of the protection level are classified but it probably provides protection against penetration of up to 14.5mm armour piercing (AP) attack through a full 360°. Protection is also provided against 155mm air burst artillery shell fragments and 9kg anti-tank mines.

The Warriors deployed to Saudi Arabia late in 1990 for Operation Granby were fitted with appliqué passive armour for increased protection. A frame is attached to either side of the hull onto which the panels of passive armour are bolted; an additional appliqué panel is installed on the glacis

In this view the wide angle periscope can be seen fitted to the driver's hatch, fully equipped with windscreen wipers. This clearly demonstrates the degree of protection provided against overhead shell fragments. The tubular metal sockets visible above the driving lights and to the right of the driver's hatch are used when rigging the camouflage netting carried by each vehicle. This Warrior belongs to the 1st Battalion, Grenadier Guards, the first unit to receive the vehicle. The guardsman in the foreground is armed with an SA80 rifle, and in this clearly posed picture is somewhat unrealistically in position in front of the vehicle. In reality he would have deployed from the rear and moved round to the sides. (MoD/CCR)

plate in front of the drivers position. No additional armour protection is provided for the engine compartment. For normal peacetime training this armour package is not fitted as it makes the vehicle wider and heavier. Appliqué armour stored since the end of the Gulf War was refitted to the British Army Warriors deployed in central Bosnia in 1992. The appliqué armour package is described in the the chapter 'Desert Storm' Modifications.

Driving the Warrior

The driver of the Warrior is seated at the front of the vehicle on the left side and is provided with an adjustable seat and a large single piece hatch cover that is hinged to the rear. When driving in the fully closed position forward observation is via a single wide angle periscope which can be quickly replaced by an image intensification periscope for night operations. For driving in the head-out position in the rain a windscreen with wiper can be rapidly fitted. When driving in the head-out position the drivers hatch cover provides protection against overhead shell fragments.

The driver steers the vehicle using a yoke type device and simply turns this which ever way he wants to go. He also has a foot brake, accelerator, parking brake and gear selector. The latter has seven positions: first reverse, second reverse, neutral, one to four, one to three, one to two and emergency first. If the driver selects one to four, for example, the transmission automatically change up or down within this gear range. Warrior has a maximum road speed of 75 km/h and accelerates from 0-48 km/h in 13.5 seconds using the forward gears and 0-48 km/h in 24 seconds using the reverse gears.

To the right of the driver is the powerpack which consists of a Perkins Engines Condor CV8 TCA four-stroke, direct injection, compression ignition 90° V-8 diesel engine developing 550 hp coupled to a X-300-4B transmission designed by the Allison Transmission Division of General Motors. In this application, the Condor has been derated but if required could deliver more power. The complete Warrior powerpack can be replaced using a crane and two men in well inside an hour under field conditions. The powerpack can also be run up outside of the vehicle on a special trolly before installation.

The Warrior has an excellent cross-country performance. However, as this photograph shows it can be a muddy ride. Crew are well-wrapped; drivers would be wearing goggles even though there is a splash plate immediately at the front of their hatch and as in many of the pictures, the rear view mirrors have been knocked out of alignment as the vehicle moves though underbrush and light woods. This view shows the turret offset to the left of the vehicle and one of the troop compartment roof hatches can be seen in the open position. Additional sockets for the camo net frame can be seen on the left of the turret. (MoD/CCR)

The V12 version of the Condor is used in all members of the Challenger 1 and Challenger 2 MBT family as well as the Scammell/Unipower Commander tank transporter, which is employed by the British Army to tow semi-trailers carrying MBTs and other AVFs from rear areas as well as taking damaged or disabled vehicles to the rear. The American transmission is manufactured under licence in the UK by Perkins Engines of Shrewsbury, which delivers the complete power-pack (engine, transmission and cooling system) to GKN Defence tested and ready for installation in the Warrior.

The X-300-4B is a fully automatic cross-drive transmission offering four forward and two reverse ranges through a torque converter and lock-up clutch. Steering is infinitely variable with true pivot turn in neutral, achieved with hydrostatically controlled double differentials. Service and parking brakes are incorporated and are hydraulically applied with mechanical backup. More recently the British-built X-300-4B transmission has been selected for installation in production versions of the Swedish Bofors/Hagglund Combat Vehicle 90 now in production for the Swedish Army.

The cooling system covers the engine, transmission, generator and vehicle brakes, the Lucas oil spray-cooled 300 Amp generator being driven from the transmission by a power take off (PTO) which also drives the hydraulic pump for the Howden Aircontrol fan. Air for cooling the powerpack is taken in and expelled through louvres on the glacis plate, the exhaust outlet being located on the forward right side of the hull.

Steering is through a hydrostatically controlled differential steer assembly, power being taken from the engine to the transmission, steering system and then through spur final drive units to the front drive sprockets. The main power assisted vehicle brakes are integral with the transmission.

From an early stage reliability was one of the key requirements of the British Army and during trials with prototype vehicles over 150,000 km were clocked up under all environmental conditions on many and varied Ministry of Defence test courses.

The turret
Mounted in the centre of the roof plate, slightly offset to the left of the vehicle's centreline is the

two-man turret of all-welded steel construction which was developed by Vickers Defence Systems under contract to GKN. The turret is mounted on a low friction roller race. The commander is seated on the right, and would normally dismount with the infantry; the gunner is seated on the left, both crewmen having a large single piece hatch cover that opens to the rear. The crew and ready ammunition are carried on a frame which rotates with the turret. Electrical supplies and communications between the turret and hull are carried by a rotary base junction of slip ring design.

Turret traverse is powered through a full 360° by the commander or gunner; handwheels are provided for emergency traverse. Weapon elevation is manual by either the commander or gunner; the latter only has manual turret traverse. A sliding screen stops any feet and legs protruding outside the turret basket and therefore being caught during traverse. These screens slide to one side to allow the turret crew to leave the vehicle via the hull. The polyethelene plastic fuel tank is located under the turret (in the prototypes the fuel tanks were in the panniers of the Warrior, one each side). The tank is partially transparent with the fuel actually visible inside. During the Gulf War it was found that the movement of the fuel was inducing a form of sea-sickness in the infantry; as a result many crews are now painting the fuel tank.

The 30mm L21A1 Rarden cannon

Main armament comprises a Royal Ordnance 30mm L21A1 Rarden cannon with a 7.62mm McDonnell Douglas Helicopter EX-34 Chain Gun (British Army designation L94A1) mounted co-axial to the left. The 30mm Rarden is also installed in the Alvis Scimitar, a member of the Scorpion family, and the Fox (4x4) Combat Vehicle Reconnaissance (Wheeled). A small num-

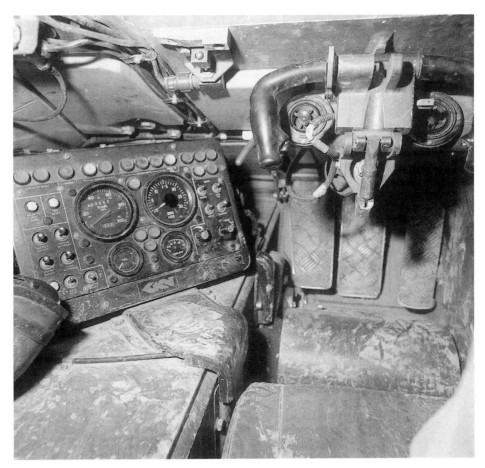

ber of FV432 APCs were fitted with a two man turret armed with a 30mm Rarden.

The Rarden cannon is a recoil-operated, self-loading weapon which is capable of firing repetitive shots and short bursts of up to six rounds (two clips of three rounds each), and has a cyclic rate of fire of 80 rounds per minute. Ammunition is fed in three round clips, the empty cartridge cases being ejected forwards out of the weapon so they do not clutter up the turret.

The weapon operates on the 'long-recoil' system in which the barrel and breech initially close together. At one point the barrel recoil ceases while the breech continues to extract the spent cartridge case, which is ejected fowards. The barrel then moves forward again, followed after an interval by the breech which loads another round.

The system on the Rarden is fully enclosed and the internal section of the weapon only protrudes 430mm into the turret space. The gun is charged by a small cocking/loading handle and no fumes can penetrate the turret area.

The Rarden was developed by the former Royal Armament Research and Development Establishment (RARDE) at Fort Halstead, and the Royal Small Arms Factory at Enfield. The latter undertook original production for the Scimitar and Fox, but as part of the UK Governments policy of competitive tendering, GKN, as the prime contractor for Warrior, held a competition, and the Warrior production contract was won by the the British Manufacture and Research Company (BMARC) of Grantham. In 1992 BMARC was taken over by Royal Ordnance and production of the Rarden was transferred to Royal Ordnance Nottingham.

As well as the ammunition shown in Table D an armour piercing discarding sabot-tracer (APDS-T) round has been developed for the Rarden, jointly developed by Royal Ordnance and

Standard production Warrior section vehicle with the two-man turret armed with a 30mm Rarden cannon and 7.62mm co-axial Chain Gun. It has had it's driving mirrors removed and also has a light weight shield over the engine grilles. The covers for the commander's and gunner's Raven roof mounted sights are both open. (GKN Defence)

PATEC of the USA. The APDS-T round has now replaced APSE-T as the main war shot for engaging enemy vehicles due to its significant increase in armour penetration.

The current production APDS-T round is the L14A2 and will penetrate over 40mm of steel armour at an incidence of 45° at ranges of over 1500m, it also has approximately half the dispersion of standard 30mm rounds. Compared with the older 30mm rounds which were originally developed by Oerlikon-Contraves of Switzerland for their KCB cannon, the more recent APDS round has a distinctive projectile with the sabot having a lateral cross-section. After leaving the barrel the sabot breaks up into four segments and falls away leaving the tungsten penetrator, which has a base tracer, to continue onto the target.

The main problem with most APDS rounds is that it is difficult for the crew to clearly observe a hit. To enable the crew to see if they have struck the target the penetrator has a pyrophoric nosecap that gives a visual indication of a hit on a hard target.

The 30mm APDS-T specifications are:

Weight of projectile	300g
Weight of cartridge case	365g
Weight complete round	822g
Muzzle velocity	1175m/s

The 7.62mm Chain Gun

The 7.62mm Chain Gun is electically fired and the most common cause of a misfire, a dud round, does not affect this weapon as the misfired round is ejected from the vehicle automatically without interrupting firing. The 7.62mm Chain Gun is also installed on a number of other British AFVs including the Challenger 2 MBT as the co-axial armament.

Empty 7.62mm cartridge cases are ejected outside of the MG, while the links are collected via a chute in the turret as with the 30mm cannon.

Unlike the Russian BMP-2 (which has a 30mm cannon) and the American Bradley (which has a 25mm cannon), the 30mm weapon of the Warrior is not stabilised so the vehicle would normally halt to open fire. For the export market, Warrior is now offered with the US Delco Systems two-man power operated turret armed with a stabilised 25mm cannon. Details of this are given in the Export Variants chapter.

The Raven sight system

Both the commander and gunner have a Pilkington PE Raven roof mounted sight which is a combined day/night sighting system that comprises three viewing channels. First a fixed focus magnified x8 day channel, second a dual field of view (x2 and x6) image intensification night channel and third a unity power day periscope. The three channels view the area under surveillance via an upper mirror, the elevation and azimuth lines of sight of which are harmonised to the bore of the 30mm main armament.

To provide the facility for main armament engagement the sight embodies three separate graticules, one in each channel, and all of these are separately adjustable in elevation and azimuth

Table B: Rarden specifications

Calibre	30mm
Overall length	3150mm
Barrel length	2438mm
Inboard length	430mm
Complete weight	110 kg
Barrel weight	24.5 kg
Rate of fire (cyclic)	80-90 rpm
Trunnion load	13.34 kN

Table C: Rarden range data

Although the 30mm Rarden cannon has a maximum effective range of 4000m, typically targets are engaged at ranges of 800 to 1500m.

Range	Elevation (mils)	Time of Flight	Residual Velocity
400m	2.0	0.39s	976m/s
1000m	5.5	1.08s	820m/s
2000m	13.7	2.59s	585m/s
3000m	27.4	4.7s	394m/s
4000m	51.4	7.71s	300m/s

Table D: Rarden ammunition

The Rarden 30mm cannon fires the following types of fixed ammunition, eg projectile and cartridge case:

Type	APSE-T	HEI-T	TP-T
Designation	L5A2	L13A1	L12A1
Weight:			
complete round	904.4g	903.9g	903.9g
projectile	357.4g	356.9g	356.9g
filling	29g	25.6g	26.5g
propellant	160g	160g	160g
Filling type	CS5390	Torpex 2	Inert
Propellant	NRN 141/RDN	NRN 141/RDN	NRN 141/RDN
Round length (complete)	285.55mm	285.55mm	285.55mm
Muzzle velocity	1070m/s	1070m/s	1070 m/s

to achieve accurate boresighting. The sights have a maximum elevation of +47° and a maximum depression of -12° and power supply is from the vehicle. The magnified day and image intensified night channels are viewed through common eyepieces with selection of day or night surveillance being effected by a single changeover lever. A focus control and light control iris are also provided in the night channel with the unity periscope viewed through a window above the eyepieces.

The gunner's and commander's Raven sights are fixed and the optics of the sight can be covered by an armoured cowl hinged at the top. A further eight periscopes give additional observation to the front, sides and rear of the turret. Typically the day sight has a detection range of 5000m and a recognition range of 3000m while the night sight has a detection range of 2500m and a recognition range of 1000 m, but these figures depend on a number of factors. In addition, mounted in the roof of the turret between the gunner's and commander's position is a split mirror periscope that can be traversed manually through 360°. The lower part folds up against the roof when not required.

The radios are mounted in the turret rear and an external stowage basket is also provided. Mounted either side of the turret is a bank of four electrically operated smoke dischargers that fire within the frontal arc of the Warrior, these being operated by the gunner as directed by the commander.

The troop compartment

The troop compartment is at the rear and is provided with a large power operated door that is hinged on the right and fitted with a single bullet proof vision block. The door can be operated from outside the vehicle, from the commanders cab or from the turret. Prototype Warriors had twin doors at the rear each with a periscope but these were difficult to open when the vehicle was on a forward slope under some tactical circumstances.

There is no provision for the infantry to fire their 5.56mm SA-80 weapons from inside of the Warrior as there was no British Army requirement for this. This option is provided for in the export Warrior vehicles. The interior of the Warrior is fitted with a spall liner which also helps to reduced noise. In the roof of the troop compartment are two rotating periscopes, one either side, these allow some of the infantry to study the outside terrain before dismounting. These are of the split mirror type and can be traversed through a full 360° and fold up against the hull roof when not required.

The infantry sit on individual padded seats that

Three close-ups of a Warrior section vehicle used by the School of Electrical and Mechanical Engineering (SEME) for driver training. Note the bank of four electrically operated smoke dischargers on the turret and the aerial mount just above and left. The aerial itself has been removed. The view of the suspension shows the six rubber-tyred road wheels and the front drive sprocket and rear idler. The three track return rollers can also just be seen. Underneath the rectangular flaps on the hull sides are the manual triggers for operating the internal Halon gas fire extinguisher system. The driver's hatch is fully open showing the integral periscope. Both the chain gun and Rarden cannon have protective covers over the muzzles. (Christopher F. Foss)

run down either side of the hull, three on the left and four on the right, each man being provided with a seat belt. The area below the seats and the area in the sponsons is used for the stowage of personnel kit and supplies. LAW-80 anti-tank weapons are stowed vertically to the left of the turret. One of the original requirements laid down by the British Army was that the Warrior should carry sufficient supplies for 48 hours of unsupported operations and this was met. The upper sides of the troop compartment slope inwards and on this is mounted a stowage box, there is an additional stowage box one either side of the hull rear. Over the roof of the troop compartment are double roof hatches that open left and right and these can be locked in the open position if required.

Other systems and equipment

Suspension is of the torsion bar type with either side having six dual squeeze formed rubber tyred aluminium road wheels with drive sprocket at the front, idler at the rear and three track-return rollers. Dampers, built into the suspension housing are fitted on the first, second and sixth road wheel stations. The integrated rotary dampers for the Warrior were designed by Horstman Defence Systems and combine the functions of an axle arm pivot and torsion bar mounting with a high performance damper to produce an integrated damper unit which is compatible with the widely accepted rotary torsion bar spring system.

This design gives over 90° of axle arm travel and a high level of controlled damping while operating temperatures remain well within acceptable limits. The suspension gives a good ride for the crew and cross-country speeds of 35km/h are normally achieved.

The road wheels of the Warrior are manufactured using GKN's squeeze formed technique having integral wear inserts and rubber rims. while the tracks fitted are of the double pin rubber-bushed cast steel type with replaceable rubber pads. The upper part of the suspension is covered by a rubber skirt which helps to keep dust down.

The fire protection system is supplied by Chubb Fire Security and uses Halon gas as the extinguising agent. Situated in the front of the vehicle, the system comprises two rechargeable Halon canisters which vent into sparge pipes running around the engine compartment. In the event of an engine fire the crew activate the system by manual triggers which release a four second burst of Halon. A second Halon canister provides the backup with further manual triggers being located externally to provide a remote fire extinguishing capability. The Warrior also carries five hand-held fire extinguishers, three of which are mounted inside the vehicle and two outside.

The electrical system is 24V and is designed to resist electro-magnetic pulses, the components being nuclear hardened. Two boiling vessels are fitted to heat rations.

Standard equipment on British Army vehicles includes a NBC system which provides a supply of uncontaminated air to all crew members via ducts, radios and crew intercom equipment. The collective NBC/Environmental Control system was developed by Howden Aircontol and is positioned on the left side of the hull with the filters being changed from outside of the troop compartment. In addition to providing protection to the crew against the effect of NBC agents it also supplies heat to the troop and crew compartment. The NBC system is operated by the gunner under instructions of the vehicle commander.

Warrior can ford to a depth of 1.3m without preparation but is not amphibious as this was not a British Army requirement.

OPERATIONAL HISTORY

The Warrior was designed to replace the FV432 APC in service with the 13 infantry battalions of the 1st, 3rd and 4th Armoured Divisions of the 1st British Corps, stationed in West Germany as one of the four corps of the Northern Army Group. The original Warrior programme called for two battalions to be equipped with Warrior each year from 1988 until 1994. During the transition period battalions equipped with FV432s would be classed as Mechanised Infantry

(Tracked) battalions, becoming Armoured Infantry battalions once equipped with Warrior. Infantry battalions stationed in the UK equipped with AT105 Saxon (4x4) wheeled APCs are designated as Mechanised Infantry (Wheeled) battalions.

In late 1987 one company of the demonstration battalion at the School of Infantry at Warminister was equipped with the Warrior for training purposes. The full conversion programme began in January 1988 with the 1st Battalion Grenadier Guards stationed at Oxford Barracks, Münster, West Germany. The Grenadiers were followed by the 1st Battalion The Staffordshire Regiment (September 1988), 1st Battalion The Royal Scots (January 1989), 3rd Battalion The Royal Regiment of Fusiliers (September 1989) and the 2nd Battalion The Royal Anglian Regiment (January 1990).

Battalion organisation
Unlike the practise in the US and West German

Infantry deploying from the rear doors of the Warrior. The reality would be that the Warrior would be shooting in the attack using its Rarden cannon. Experience in the Gulf was that infantry stayed on board the vehicles as much as possible and the vehicles fought through the position; deploying from an armoured vehicle makes the infantry vulnerable and can slow down the attack. The power operated door at the rear of the troop compartment has one vision block, in this case with the internal cover in place. One of the rotating periscopes in the roof of the troop compartment is visible, the other being obscured by the left roof hatch. Also visible is one of the externally mounted fire extinguishers. The other is to the left of the driver's hatch. (MoD/CCR)

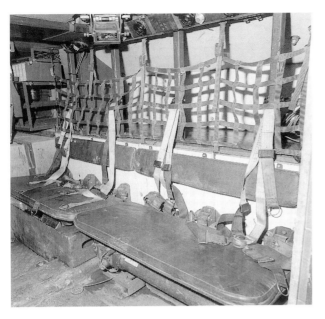

The right hand side of the troop compartment showing the harness for the troops, and the additional stowage space for personal kit behind the seats. The straps holding the netting in place have quick-release catches. One of the two split-mirror rotating periscopes is visible in the roof; the other is above the left hand bench.

A close-up view of the storage space under the seats in the troop compartment. Here we see additional ammunition for the crews small arms (SA80 and LSW) stored under the two-man bench on the right hand side of the compartment. The bar in front of the seat is part of the mechanism of the power operated door.

armies of dedicating infantry battalions to specific roles, British infantry battalions are periodically rotated between roles with the longest tour being the four years served by battalions as mechanised infantry in Germany. The complexity and cost of training battalions to be proficient in the Warrior role resulted in the length of tour in Germany being extended to six years.

Armoured Infantry battalions were initially issued with 52 Warriors. One command variant was provided for the battalion commanding officer and two for the headquarters of the fire support company. The three rifle companies each received 14 Warriors: two command variants for company headquarters, while the three rifle platoons each received one Warrior section vehicle for platoon headquarters and one section vehicle for each of the three rifle sections. The battalion's Royal Electrical and Mechanical Engineer (REME) light aid detachment was allocated three Warrior Repair and four Warrior Recovery variants.

The high cost of Warrior prevented a complete replacement of all AFVs in infantry service. The

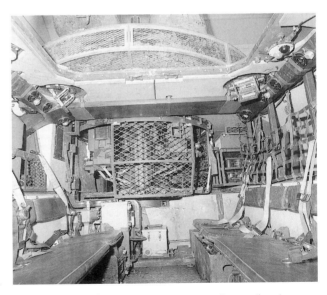

The interior of the troop compartment showing the padded benches for the seven infantry, three on the left, four on the right. The farthest seat on the left is the NBC toilet. The roof hatches are open and the two rotating roof periscopes can be seen to the left and right. The mesh screen on the turret basket slides to the left to give the crew access to the troop compartment.

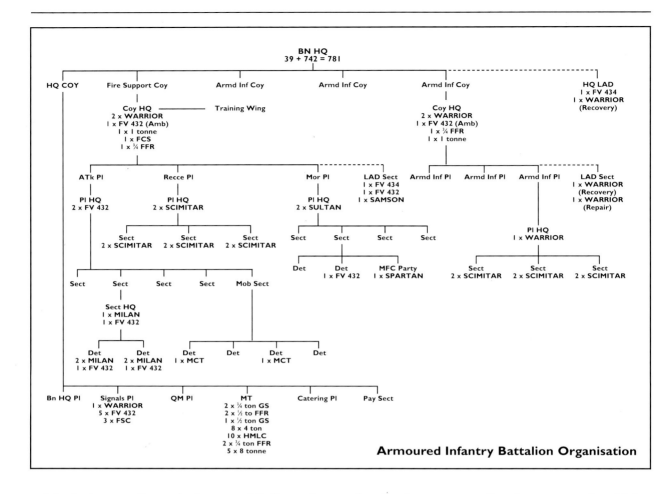

Armoured Infantry Battalion Organisation

original plan was for each Armoured Infantry battalion to retain 38 FV430 series vehicles and 19 vehicles of the Combat Vehicle Reconnaissance (Tracked) series. The anti-tank platoon would retain 14 FV432s to transport its 20 Milan ATGWs while its mobile section was equipped with four CVR(T) Spartans with Milan Compact Turrets. The reconnaissance platoon would remain equipped with eight CVR(T) Scimitars armed with 30mm Rarden cannons. The mortar platoon continued to operate its eight 81mm mortars from FV432s directed by four mortar fire control parties mounted in CVR(T) Spartans and commanded by a platoon headquarters in two CVR(T) Sultans.

On the transition from the Mechanised Infantry (Tracked) to the Armoured Infantry role a battalion's establishment was increased to provide a second Captain in each rifle company, a second Sergeant for each of the nine rifle platoons, and

nine Rarden gunners for the command vehicles. The disappearance of the threat from the Warsaw Pact following the collapse of Communism in Eastern Europe was to have a profound effect on the British Army. In July 1990 plans were announced to reduce regular army strength from 156,000 to about 120,000 and halve the number of troops stationed in Germany. Before these plans could be detailed attention was diverted to the Iraqi invasion of Kuwait on 2 August 1990 which led to the largest deployment of British armoured forces since 1945.

Desert Storm

On 14 September 1990 it was announced that the 7th Armoured Brigade would be transported from its bases in Germany to Saudi Arabia to join American, French and other coalition forces. The brigade was armour heavy with two Challenger 1 MBT regiments, namely The Royal Scots

Dragoon Guards (RSDG) and The Queen's Royal Irish Hussars (QRIH), and only one armoured infantry battalion, the 1st Battalion, The Staffordshire Regiment (1 Staffords). The brigade was selected because it was the first to be fully equipped and trained with the Challenger 1 MBT and the Warrior. The Staffords, which had been equipped with Warrior in 1988, had undertaken an intensive period of training at the British Army Training Unit Suffield (BATUS) in Alberta, Canada, during June and July 1990.

On 22 November the British government announced that the British deployment, code-named Operation 'Granby', would be expanded with the despatch of the 4th Armoured Brigade and divisional troops to form the 1st (British) Armoured Division under the command of Major General Rupert Smith. The 4th Armoured Brigade was infantry heavy with two armoured infantry battalions, 1st Battalion, The Royal Scots (1 RS) and 3rd Battalion, The Royal Regiment of Fusiliers (3 RRF), and one armoured regiment the 14th/20th King's Hussars (14/20 KH).

For 'Desert Storm' the establishment of the armoured infantry battalions was increased to 875. Five infantry battalions provided reinforcements for 1 Staffords, the largest contingent being two

Warrior section vehicles fitted with Chobham armour during training in Saudi Arabia before the start of Operation 'Desert Storm' and therefore without recognition signs. In addition to the ceramic armour along the side the vehicles have added armour to the glacis plate and the crews personal kit can be seen stowed on mud guards to the front. In the background is a 4-tonner fuel vehicle with 3 fuel cells on it. (GKN Defence)

officers, four infantry sections and 16 Warrior gunners from the 1st Battalion Grenadier Guards, the first battalion to be trained on Warrior. One complete Grenadier company reinforced 1 RS while another company joined 3 RRF. Training which had begun on the NATO range complex in northern Germany was continued in Saudi Arabia, culminating with live fire exercises at brigade level and two major divisional exercises. To improve the mobility of the Warrior battalions, which still employed 38 FV432 APCs as 81 mm mortar carriers, Milan section carriers, ambulances and REME vehicles, the number of Warriors in each battalion was increased from 53 to 69. The additional Warriors replaced FV432s in the anti-tank platoons and the CVR(T) Spartans of the mortar fire control parties.

Within the brigades the British Army's standard practise of grouping tank squadrons and infantry companies with supporting sub-units to form either armoured infantry or armoured battle groups was followed. For example 1 Staffords regrouped to form the 1 Staffords Battle Group which included the RSDG's 'B' Squadron and the QRIH's 'C' Squadron, while the battalion's 'A' Company was attached to the RSDG Battle Group. Since the replacement of the FV432 by the Warrior, with its better protection and 30mm Rarden cannon, the practice of mingling infantry platoons and armoured troops to form 'combat teams' was abandoned in favour of complete armoured squadrons and armoured infantry companies operating together as 'squadron/company groups' for a specific mission.

The ground offensive to recapture Kuwait began on 24 February 1991 (G Day). Riding in the troop compartments of their Warriors infantrymen wore their Nuclear, Biological and Chemical (NBC) suits and the newly issued combat body armour vests. On the night of G+1 the Staffords' 'A' Company, part of the RSDG Battle Group, executed the first armoured infantry attackagainst enemy positions on objective Copper. Supported by the 120mm guns of the Challengers and their own 30mm Rarden cannons, 'A' Company repeatedly dismounted from their Warriors amid rain and sandstorms to clear enemy positions with small arms fire and grenades. The position was overrun in a little over 90 minutes with only three Staffords wounded.

Over the follwoing two days 1 STAFFORDS battle group and those of QRIH and RSDG made a series of armoured infantry assaults onto enemy positions on objectives Zinc, Platinum 1, Platinum 2 and Lead.

The ceasefire came into effect at 0800, 28 February 1991 with 1 STAFFORDS, QRIH and RSDG all in position on objective Cobalt asrtide the Basra road. No Warriors had been lost to enemy action. One Warrior in 1 Staffords Battle Group was hit by a 120mm High Explosive Squash Head (HESH) round accidentally fired by a RSDG Challenger which hit a Chobham armour plate only denting the Warrior's hull beneath. In another tragic case of mistaken identity two Warriors of the 3 RRF Battle Group were destroyed, with the loss of nine dead and one

British armour in the Gulf: Warrior mechanised combat vehicles on the left and Vickers Defence Systems Challenger 1 MBTs on the right. Note the extensive stowage on virtually all vehicles and the red panels as an aid to visual recognition from the air. The crew are wearing NBC clothing and the photograph was probably taken after the fighting against Iraq was over, because the vehicles are not in any tactical formation, but the presence of aerial recognition panels and the fact that the crews are still wearing NBC equipment suggests that this was probably a few days after the fighting ended when the possible threat of an NBC attack still existed. (MoD/CCR)

wounded, by Maverick missiles fired by US Air Force A-10 Thunderbolt II aircraft. For their efforts to rescue the wounded, Fusilier Simon Bakkor and Sergeant Trevor Smith, a Royal Anglian attached to C company RRF, were awarded the Queen's gallantry medal.

The Warrior's role today
In the months following the end of the war, as the 1st Armoured Division's Warriors and other equipment were shipped back to Germany and the UK, details of the army's future organisation were

finalised. The shape of 'Britain's Army for the Nineties' was announced in July 1991. Strength would be cut to 116,000 by 1997 and the number of infantry battalions reduced from 55 to 38, although in February 1993 this was revised to 119,000 and 40 infantry battalions. Instead of 13 battalions, only eight battalions will now be equipped with Warrior.

Bosnia-Herzcegovina

In 1992 the British government took the decision to contribute an armoured infantry battle group to the United Nations Protection Force (UNPRO-FOR) in Bosnia-Herzcegovina. As in the Gulf war additional armour was fitted to the Warriors before the UN's white livery was applied. Designed for high intensity armoured combat the Warriors are employed in the unanticipated role of protecting the distribution of food and medical aid and the safe passage of refugee convoys. In this work, one Warrior is reported to have taken a hit by an RPG 7 on its ceramic side armour with no penetration or damage to the vehicle or armour.

In April 1993 the 1st Battalion, The Cheshire Regiment completed the first six month tour and was relieved by the 1st Battalion, The Prince of Wales's Own Regiment of Yorkshire. At the same time 45 Warriors, which had already covered 10,000km in the Gulf, were rotated to ensure even wear across the fleet. From the desert sands of Kuwait to the mountain roads of Bosnia the Warrior has proven to be everything the British Army had hoped for since the appearance of the first infantry fighting vehicles in the early 1970s. The uncertainties of the post-Cold War world are likely to ensure continued service for the Warrior.

BRITISH ARMY VARIANTS

The vehicles covered here are those other than the standard British Army Section Vehicle.

Command Vehicles

The British Army deploys three command ver-sions of the Warrior: platoon, company and battal-ion. These are essentially the same as the section vehicle with the same two-man turret but have a different communications fit for each role. GKN fit the harness, but the communications equip-ment is fitted by the Army at depot-level before the vehicles are issued to the regiments. Command Vehicles also have map boards and are recognised externally by their additional radio antennas and a different rear hull. The standard section vehicle has a single power-operated door while the command vehicles have double doors similar to those on the original section vehicle prototype that open left and right.

Mechanised Recovery Vehicle (Repair) (FV513)

The first two prototypes were completed in 1986 and following trials it was accepted for service with REME. The initial production vehicles were completed in 1990 with the original British Army requirement being for a total of 67 vehicles, but this was subsequently reduced to 39 vehicles as a result of 'Options for Change'. This version has a five-man crew consisting of commander/gunner, driver, and three fitters. Mounted on the left side of the hull is a hydraulically operated crane with a telescopic jib which can lift a maximum load of 6500kg and has a maximum reach of 4.52m. The crane can be traversed through a full 360° and before the crane is used a hydraulically operated stabiliser leg is lowered to the ground. The crane enables complete Challenger 1, Challenger 2 or Warrior powerpacks to be quickly changed in the field.

Mounted in the rear of the Warrior MRV(R) is a hydraulically operated winch with a capacity of 20,000kg which can be increased to 38,000kg when double-reeved with sufficient cable to enable a single line pull of 100m. A pilot winch is fitted as standard and this has 200m of cable with a capacity of 1250kg and is also used to raise and lower the large earth anchor mounted at the rear of the vehicle. A suspension lockout system is fit-ted to provide a more stable platform when lifting or recovery operations are in progress.

Standard equipment includes an air compressor for the use of air tools and to assist in field

This Warrior has extensive modification. The rear deck is covered with CARM (Chemical Agent Resistant Material.) – a plastic sheeting which was used to protect vehicles against possible chemical attack. Just visible on the crews' shoulders is the Desert Rat insignia of 7 Armoured Brigade but the picture was probably set up for the photographer because on the in-flight stowage rack on the side armour can be seen one of the crews personal stereo kits which would have been stowed away if the vehicle was in action. In the front of the vehicle by the extra armour on the glassis plate is an oil drum and additional personal kit, and shovels and digging equipment can be seen tucked in along the hull side behind the additional armour. (MoD/CCr)

repairs. An electro-hydraulic pump allows the vehicle to change its own powerpack in the field should this be required.

The Warrior MRV(R) is fitted with a GKN Defence designed one man manually operated turret armed with the same 7.62mm L94A1 Chain Gun as fitted as the co-axial weapon to the standard Warrior section vehicle. It has a collective NBC system and and air-conditioning system.

Mechanised Combat Repair Vehicle (MCRV) (FV512)

This is virtually identical to the Warrior Mechanised Recovery Vehicle (Repair) previously described, but does not have the rear mounted earth anchor or winch so has no recovery capability. The original British Army requirement was for 110 vehicles, later reduced to 103.

If required, the Warrior MCRV can tow the specially developed GKN Defence T4 high mobility trailer which weighs 10,500kg fully loaded and can carry a complete Challenger 1 or Challenger 2 MBT powerpack. This trailer employs a four-damper jacking system to maintain a safe level platform when not connected for towing. A total of 45 have been supplied to the British Army for use with the Warrior MCRV.

Mechanised Artillery Observation Vehicle (MAOV)

This is the most complex version of the Warrior family of vehicles and was developed specifically

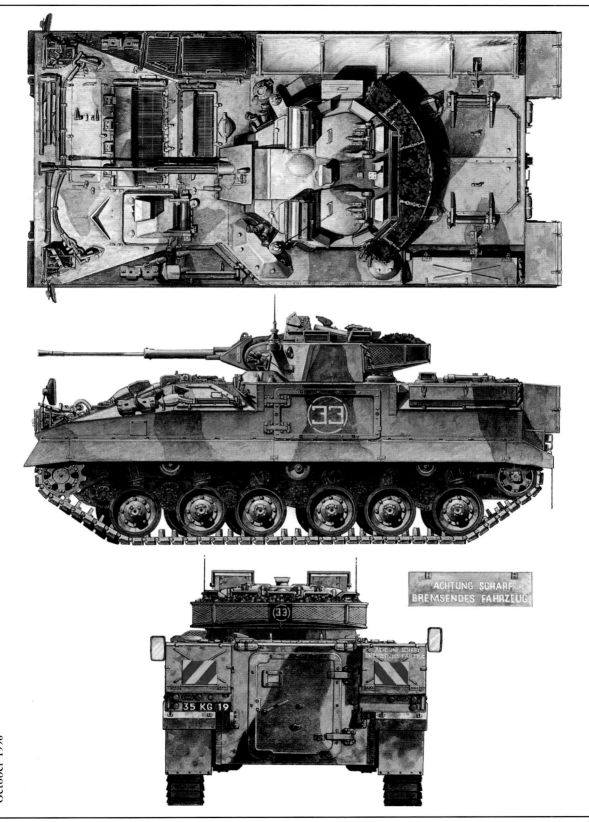

Section vehicle, BAOR, NORTHAG, Germany, October 1990

ACHTUNG SCHARF
BREMSENDES FAHRZEUG

35 KG 19

A

Section vehicle, 1st Bn., The Staffordshire Regt., southern Iraq, Operation 'Desert Sabre', 25 February 1991

B

Section vehicle, C Coy., 1st Bn., the 22nd (Cheshire) Regt., 1 Cheshire battle group, Vitez, Bosnia, January 1993

C

WARRIOR SECTION VEHICLE
2nd Bn., Royal Anglian Regt., Celle, Germany, March 1994

SPECIFICATIONS

Crew: 3 + 7
Combat weight: 25,700kg
Power-to-weight ratio: 21.4 bhp/tonne
Ground pressure: 0.65kg/cm^2
Length: 6.34m
Width: 3.034m
Height: 2.791m
Ground clearance: 0.49m
Track width: 460mm
Max. speed (road): 75km/h
Acceleration (0-48km/h): 13.5s
Fuel capacity: 770 litres
Best cruising speed: 60km/h
Max. range: 660km at cruising speed
Fording depth: 1.3m
Engine: Perkins Engines CV8 TCA V-8 diesel, developing 550 hp at 2300 rpm
Transmission: Allison X-300-4B, 4 forwards and 2 reverse gears
Main armament: 1 x 30mm Rarden cannon
Co-axial armament: 1 x 7.62mm Chain Gun
Smoke laying equipment: 2 x 4 smoke dischargers
Ammunition: 250 x 30mm, 2000 x 7.62mm
Muzzle velocity: 1070 m/s
Max. effective range: 4000 m
Gun stabiliser: no
Gun elevation/depression: +45°/-10°

KEY

1. Rarden 30mm cannon
2. 7.62mm Hughes chain gun
3. Engine air intake
4. Radio aerial
5. Armoured shutter for Commander's sight
6. Smoke dischargers
7. Commander's Raven sight
8. Breech of Rarden cannon
9. Commander's services box
10. Ready ammo storage
11. Commander's seat
12. Gunner's hand traverse
13. VRC 353 radio
14. Gunner's seat
15. Turret bustle cage
16. Troop compartment periscope
17. Troop compartment roof hatch
18. Padded troop seats
19. Stowage for personal equipment and 94mm LAW
20. Rear stowage bins
21. Bullet proof vision block
22. Power operated door
23. Track guard
24. Rear idler
25. Track with rubber pads
26. Hydraulic ram for rear door
27. Rubber side skirt
28. Road wheels
29. Stowage space under seat
30. Chemical toilet (NBC environment)
31. Boiling vessel
32. NBC system
33. Return roller
34. Armoured door to NBC system
35. Driver's adjustable seat
36. Gear range selector
37. Driver's instrument panel
38. Accelerator
39. Emergency brake
40. Brake
41. Final drive
42. Sockets for cam set poles
43. Lifting eye
44. Driver's steering column
45. Driver's hatch
46. Drivers periscope

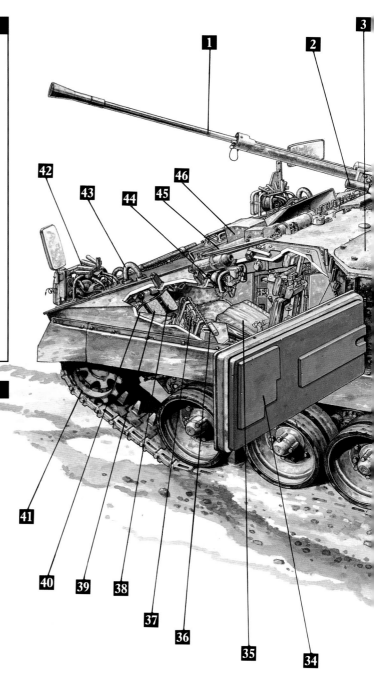

D

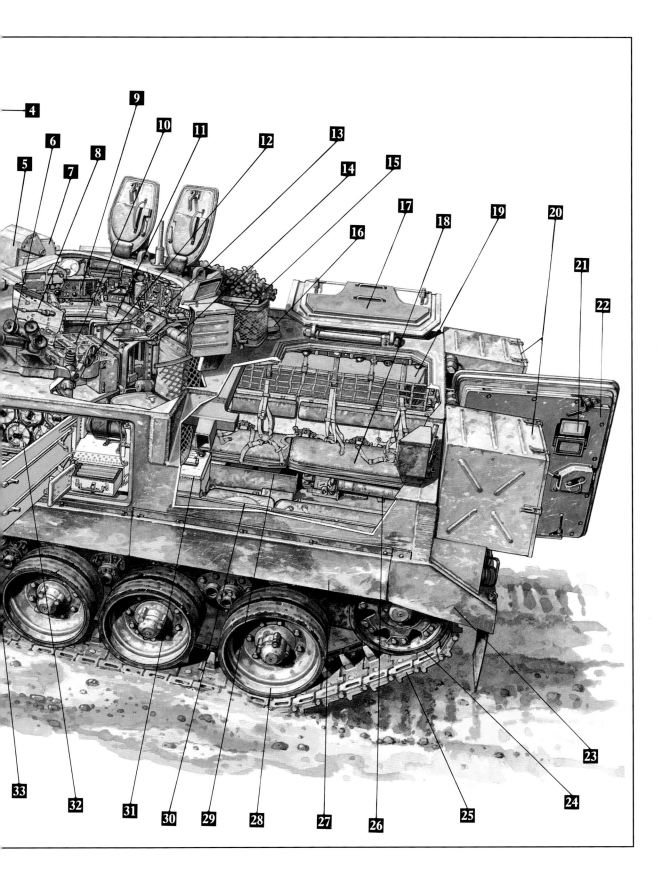

1: Mechanised Recovery Vehicle (Repair), 1st (British) Armoured Division,
Operation Granby, Saudi Arabia, February 1991

2: Mechanised Combat Repair Vehicle,
BAOR, NORTHAG, Germany, October 1990

E

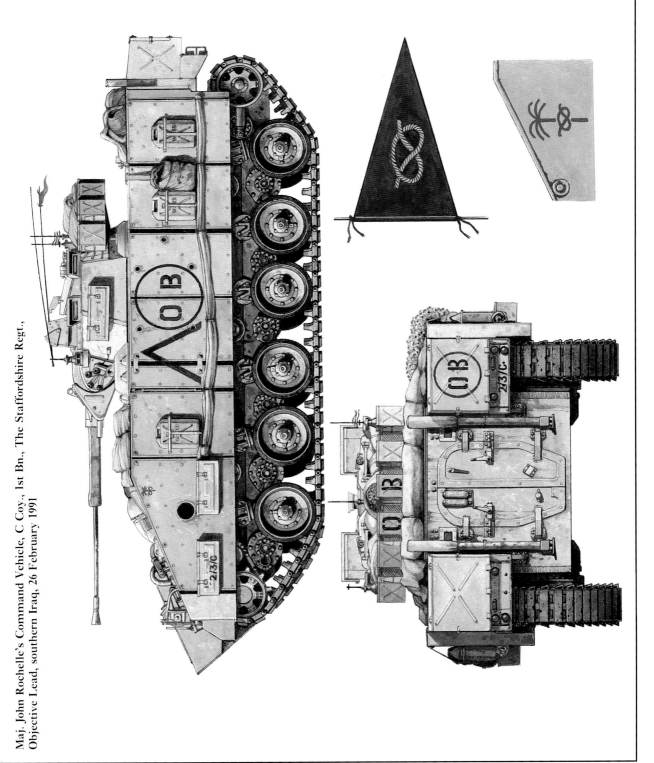

Maj. John Rochelle's Command Vehicle, C Coy., 1st Bn., The Staffordshire Regt.,
Objective Lead, southern Iraq, 26 February 1991

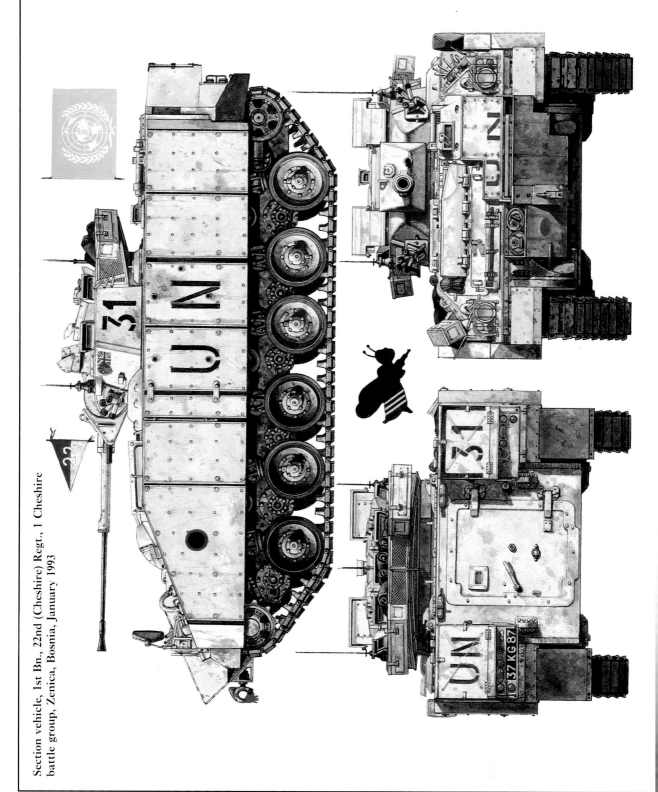

Section vehicle, 1st Bn., 22nd (Cheshire) Regt., 1 Cheshire battle group, Zenica, Bosnia, January 1993

G

The commander's (right) side of the turret of a Warrior Command vehicle, showing the Raven roof mounted sight, two of the eight turret periscopes and to the right of the commander's position below the turret ring storage space for additional ammunition.

to meet the requirements of the British Royal Artillery. The Warrior MAOV is used by the forward observation officers and battery commanders of Royal Artillery field regiments. The first prototype was completed in 1988 followed by the first production vehicles in 1990.

Externally the vehicle is very similiar to the Warrior section vehicle but has a dummy 30mm Rarden cannon and a six-man crew consisting of driver, two observers in the turret (one of whom commands the vehicle) and three men in the rear to operate the communications equipment and the Thorn EMI MSTAR battlefield surveillance radar.

The observer has a Pilkington PE Osprey combined day/thermal/laser system which has magnifications of x1 and x8 in the day mode and built in laser protection. The thermal imaging system is based on the GEC Avionics Class II Thermal Imaging Common Modules already in service with

With its additional radio aerials this Warrior MOAV looks deceptively like a command vehicle from this angle. The commander has a Pilkington PE Osprey sight and the other observer the standard Raven sight. This variant was first used by the Royal Artillery during Operation 'Desert Storm'. (GKN Defence)

A scene typical of the early days in the desert. The vehicles have not been up-armoured with additional plates so this is probably late 1990. The vehicle on the left is identifiable as a Stafford Warrior by the unofficial 'Afrika Korps'-style Stafford Knot insignia on the rear stowage bins. The crew are wearing a mixture of the standard desert pattern camouflage kit, but also temperate DPM clothing. Extremes of temperature are common in desert regions and as the weather deteriorated in Saudi Arabia frost was not uncommon. Some of the vehicles had hessian scrim along the hull sides to drop down over the tracks when they were camouflaged up. (GKN Defence)

What appears to be a pair of 7th Armoured Brigade vehicles, a Mechanised Recovery Vehicle (Repair) on the left and a Mechanised Combat Repair Vehicle to the right. Confusingly the MRV(R) has the Desert Rat painted in both red and black on the hull side. The MRV(R) appears to be replacing the powerpack of the MCRV. Note the stabiliser lowered at the left rear of the vehicle and the crane jib extended. (GKN Defence)

the British Army. The assistant has a Pilkington PE Raven day/night sight which is fitted as standard to the Section Warrior. Between the observer's and assistant's position is a remote display for the thermal imaging system.

The vehicle is also fitted with an inertial land navigation and attitude reference system, Marconi Radar and Control Systems BATES (Battlefield Artillery Target Engagement System) and extensive communications equipment.

Mounted to the rear of the turret, on an arm, is the Thorn EMI Manportable Surveillance and Target Acquisition Radar (MSTAR) which entered service with the British Army in 1990. For maximum coverage this is raised on its mast but if required by the tactical situation it can also be deployed away from the vehicle.

Battery Command Vehicle (BCV)
This was also developed to meet the requirements of the Royal Artillery, the first production vehicles being completed in 1990. Each RA field regiment

This 7th Armoured Brigade Warrior MRV(R) is clearly recovering a vehicle in what is more than likely a training exercise to test the tow-capabilities of the vehicle.

The two crew give a good indication of the large size of the vehicle. Interestingly, one of them is wearing standard olive drab coveralls. (GKN Defence)

would have one of these vehicles per battery.

Dozer/mine clearing
The Warrior can be fitted with the Pearson Engineering front-mounted Surface Mine Plough (SMP) or the Pearson Combat Dozer Blade UDK-2. Developed by Pearson Engineering to meet the British Army Staff Requirement 3916 the SMP is a multi-section, multi-bladed V-Plough that physically removes mines from the path of the vehicle, pushing them to one side. The combination of the articulated blades and the in-built hydraulic system enables the plough to conform to the actual ground conditions so maintaining blade contact with the surface.

The blades of the SMP are articulated in such

Warrior MRV(R) Specifications

Crew	5
Combat weight	30,000kg
Length overall	6.675m
Width:	3.13m
Height over cupola	2.302m
Height over roof	1.935m
Ground clearance	0.49m
Max road speed	71km/h
Max road range	500km
Angle of approach/departure	29/34.5
Armament	1 × 7.62mm Chain Gun
Ammunition	4000 × 7.62mm
Smoke dischargers	up to 8 banks

(Other specifications as per standard Warrior)

a way that they are able to ride up and over small obstacles without damage. The 18-blade version of the SMP weighs only 1150kg and is 4.16m wide and can clear a path to a maximum width of 3.14m. In addition to the Warrior MCV, it can also be fitted to the FV432 APC, members of the Combat Vehicle Reconniassance (Tracked) family and a 4 tonne (4x4) truck.

The UDK-2 is a smaller and lighter version of the Pearson UDK-1 originally developed for the Challenger 1 MBT and can be quickly fitted to a number of AFVs including the Warrior. It is typically used to clear battlefield obstacles and prepare firing positions for other vehicles.

Warrior with Milan

This is the latest version of the Warrior to enter service with the British Army and was developed for Operation 'Desert Storm'.

The Euromissile Milan ATGW launcher is pintle mounted on the right side of the turret roof with racks being provided internally for additional missiles. As the Milan can be fitted with a thermal night sight, this version has a significant advantage over the standard Warrior which only has image intensification night vision equipment fitted. Milan was manufactured under licence for the British Army by British Aerospace Dynamics (BAeD).

Late in 1991 the MoD ordered another batch of Warriors, believed to number about 100 vehicles, to carry Milan. Previously this role was carried out by the FV432 APC which, as was demonstrated in Operation 'Desert Storm', clearly lacks the battlefield mobility to support the Warrior in action.

Warrior with Trigat

Today the British Army uses two ATGWs in the ground based role: Milan with a maximum range of 2000m and the BAeD Swingfire with a maximum range of 4000m. Both of these wire-guided missiles have a HEAT (High Explosive Anti-Tank) warhead.

The Milan is employed in three configurations: normal tripod mounted for use by infantry, pintle mounted on a FV432 APC or Warrior (scheduled to replace the FV432 in this role), and the Alvis Spartan with Milan Compact Turret.

The Milan will be replaced later this decade by the Euromissile Dynamics Group (EMDG) Trigat Medium Range missile system which will be deployed in the normal tripod role and vehicle mounted on the Warrior MCV.

The Warrior can be fitted with a one-man power operated turret armed with a 7.62mm MG and fitted with a day/night sighting system. Pods of two Trigat MRs are mounted either side of the turret and additional missiles are carried internally to allow the system to be manually reloaded. A standard infantry tripod mount can be carried to enable the system to be deployed away from the vehicle if required.

TRIGAT MR has a maximum range of around 2500m and is fitted with a tandem warhead fitted with an infrared stand-off fuse. Guidance is by Optical Beam Riding (OBR) of a coded infrared (IR) laser beam. All the gunner has to do is to keep the sight on target to ensure a hit.

EXPORT VARIANTS

In addition to the extensive range of vehicles developed to meet the specific operational requirements of the British Army, GKN Defence have, using the same basic chassis, developed a wide range of vehicles specifically for the export market.

A Warrior from 1st Battalion the Cheshires escorting a convoy somewhere in Bosnia as part of Operation Grapple. This is obviously in the early days of the operation as this vehicle is flying a Union Jack, a practice that has since been abandoned. There is very little in terms of external stowage on these vehicles as they are operating from a relatively secure base. (Soldier Magazine)

Desert Warrior

For a vehicle such as Warrior, the Middle East is by far the biggest potential market as most NATO countries normally develop their own infantry combat vehicles. Early examples of the standard British Army Warrior were demonstrated in a number of countries in Europe and the Middle East before it was decided to develop the Desert Warrior, which is adapted to meet the different operational and environmental requirements of this region.

Desert Warrior has no less than 27 amendments to the standard British Army specification, including a combined air-conditioning and NBC filtration unit and specially designed front and rear flaps that help ensure the dust plume is kept to a minimum even when the vehicle is driven at speed.

Desert Warrior is fitted with the American Delco Systems Operations two-man power-operated turret which is similiar to that fitted to the Canadian built Light Armored Vehicle 25 (LAV-25). The two man turret is of all-welded steel armour construction that provides protection matched to that of the chassis with the commander seated on the right and the gunner on the left. Both have a large single piece hatch cover that opens to the rear, and adjustable seats.

The commander has seven M27 unity perisopes for all-round observation and an M36E1 sight for aiming the main armament while the gunner has an M27 unity periscope to his left and a M36E1 sight to his right for aiming the main and secondary armament. The M36E1 sight is provided with a day channel with a magnification of x7 and a 10° field of view, passive night image intensifier channel with a magnification of x8 and an 8° field of view and a unity channel with 60° horizontal and 10° vertical field of view. The M36E1 sight can be replaced by other sights such as the Delco Improved M36 sight (DIM36), Delco LAV-25 thermal sight, Hughes GITS, DIM36 with integrated laser rangefinder and the Delco LAV-25 thermal sight with laser rangefinder. The thermal night capability offers a number of significant operational advantages over the older image intensification night sights as targets can be recognised out to 2000m under virtually any weather conditions. The LAV-25 sight utilises the Hughes Infrared Equipment (HIRE) thermal sub-system and contains accurate stadia and ballistic reticles for both wide and narrow fields of view. This is fully compatible with the existing M36E1 sight and uses a binocular video viewer or remote cathode ray tube (CRT) display which is fully operable from the commander's position.

Turret traverse and weapon elevation is of the electrically driven hydraulic pump type and both the commander and gunner are provided with hand controllers. Manual controls are fitted for emergency use. The turret traverses through a full 360° and weapons can elevate from -8° to + 60°.

This two-man turret is armed with the combat proven McDonnell-Douglas 25mm M242 Chain Gun. Unlike the Rarden cannon on British Army Warrior the 25mm Chain Gun is stabilised and the Desert Warrior can thus engage and hit targets while moving.

Mounted co-axial with the main armament is a 7.62mm M240 MG and mounted on either side of the turret firing fowards is a bank of four M243 electrically operated smoke dischargers. If required the Desert Warrior can have a 7.62mm M240 MG mounted on the turret roof for local and anti-aircraft defence.

Hughes TOW missile launcher tubes can be mounted either side of the turret. This optional system, which gives the Warrior DFV the capability to engage enemy armour out to a range of 3750m, has an integrated Hughes sight that provides both thermal imaging and TOW tracking. When not required the TOW launcher folds down through 90° alongside the turret. Once the TOW

missiles have been fired new rounds would be loaded manually by one of the rear crew members through the roof hatch. If required the Delco Systems Operations turret can be delivered with the electrical harness fitted to enable the TOW system to be fitted at a later date.

As well as the driver, commander and gunner, Desert Warrior carries seven infantrymen in the rear: four down the right side and three down the left. If required a total of five firing ports and associated vision devices and fume extractors can be fitted in the rear troop compartment; two in either side and one in the rear door. The main drawback with the installation of firing ports is that they reduce the amount of space on board for the stowage of essential equipment. As Desert Warrior has been designed to operate in high ambient temperatures a combined high performance air-conditioning and NBC system is fitted as standard.

Optional equipment for Desert Warrior includes a roof mounted laser detector (to warn the crew when the vehicle is being illuminated by a laser designator or rangefinder), various radio systems, land navigation system (including Global Positioning System) and a battlefield surveillance radar.

This group of Warriors from 1 Cheshire battle group are preparing to leave the unit's main base at Vitez. All the vehicles do appear to be carrying lubrication oil stowed at the front next to the additional armour plate. The vehicle in the foreground seems to have a cooker unit mounted above the oil. It appears to be the side walls of the burner for cooking in the field. This may be precaution against long delays while on escort duty. (Soldier Magazine)

The crew of this vehicle seem very relaxed although Warriors escorting supply convoys in Bosnia have repeatedly come under fire from snipers and mortars. Normally this is a result of being caught in the crossfire between the warring factions but occasionally the fire has been directed at the troops themselves. The only fatality suffered by a Warrior crew occurred on 14 January 1993 when L/Cpl. Wayne Edwards was killed. While escorting an ambulance the vehicle he was in was caught in the crossfire of a fierce clash between Muslim and Croat forces near Gorni Vakuf. (Soldier Magazine)

Following extensive trials, Kuwait selected the GKN Desert Warrior in preference to the US FMC Corporation M2 Bradley infantry fighting vehicle in late 1992. GKN confirmed the £500 million Kuwaiti order for 250 Desert Warriors in August 1993. Production is expected to begin in early 1994.

Arctic Warrior

The Arctic variant is similiar to Desert Warrior although it does not have the TOW missile system installed but is fitted with a high performance integrated diesel air-to-air heater instead of the standard air-conditioning system.

PROTOTYPE VARIANTS

The following variants have only reached the prototype stage, or have been paper studies only. As of mid-1993, none of these vehicles had entered production.

APC 90

Proposed by GKN Defence in the early days of the programme, APC 90 was a shortened Warrior with five road wheels either side and fitted with a cupola mounted 7.62mm machine gun.

Warrior with CM 90 turret

In mid-1984 a Warrior was demonstrated fitted with a Belgian Cockerill CM 90 two-man power-operated turret armed with a Cockerill 90mm Mk III gun, 7.62mm co-axial MG, OIP computerised fire control system and Cadillac Gage Textron two-axis stabilisation system.

Warrior with C25 turret

The Warrior has also been demonstrated fitted with the Belgian Cockerill C25 two-man power operated turret armed with a Oerlikon-Contraves 25mm KBB cannon, 7.62mm co-axial MG and a stabilisation system.

Warrior with HOT ATGW

For demonstration purposes, a Warrior had its normal turret removed and replaced by the Euromissile HOT Compact Turret (HCT), with four HOT ATGWs in the ready to launch position and a further 14 missiles carried in the hull. The latter would be manually loaded through the rear roof hatches.

Warrior Mechanised Combat Repair Vehicle in travelling configuration with stabiliser leg at left rear raised and hydraulic crane traversed to the front of the vehicle. (GKN Defence)

The one-man turret's powered traverse could turn 30° left and right with powered elevation from -18° to +23° with the operator having a day sight with a magnification of x3 and x12. This version was first shown in public late in 1982 but was never adopted and Euromissile is no longer marketing this turret.

Low profile Warrior
Unveiled at the 1988 British Army Equipment Exhibition was the low profile Warrior chassis armed with the Oerlikon-Contraves ADATS air defence system, which has eight missiles in the ready to launch position.

This low profile chassis could be used for a number of proposed versions, including a light tank with a three-man power operated turret mounted on the hull at the rear. This would be armed with a 105mm gun and fitted with day/night sights, a computerised fire control system and a gun stabilisation system. The overall height of the low profile version of Warrior (to the hull top without turret or weapons installed) is only 1.6m.

Warrior Engineer
This proposed variant for combat engineers features a one-man turret armed with a 7.62mm machine gun. A Thorn EMI Ranger anti-person-nel scatter mine system could be fitted onto the roof at the rear and the vehicle could also tow an anti-tank mine laying system such as the Royal Ordnance Bar system. Another engineer vehicle is fitted with a telescopic arm which is mounted on top of the hull towards the rear, this can be fitted with various attachments such as a bucket or auger.

Warrior Anti-tank
In addition to the Warrior equipped with Milan adopted by the British Army after the Gulf War and Warrior with the HCT previously mentioned, studies by GKN have shown that the Warrior chassis can be fitted with a wide range of ATGWs such as the Hughes TOW.

Warrior Anti-aircraft (gun)
The chassis can be fitted with various types of anti-aircraft gun turrets including the French Thomson-CSF Sabre armed with twin 30mm cannon and a tracking/surveillance radar.

Warrior Anti-aircraft (missile)
The chassis can be fitted with various types of surface-to-air missile systems including Rapier and Roland. It was one of the contenders for the platform for the Shorts Starstreak High Velocity SAM developed to meet the requirements of the

Warrior Mechanised Combat Repair Vehicle towing a GKN Defence T4 high mobility trailer which can carry a complete power-pack for the Challenger 1 or 2 MBT or Warrior. (GKN Defence)

Royal Artillery, but the British Army subsequently adopted the Alvis Stormer chassis instead.

Warrior Mortar
The British Army still uses the FV432 fitted with a Royal Ordnance 81mm turntable mounted mortar. The Warrior can be fitted with various 81mm and 120mm mortar systems. These include the Royal Ordnance 120mm turret mounted mortar and a turret mounted French Thomson-Brandt 81mm mortar.

Warrior Rocket Launcher
The Warrior chassis could be adopted to take various types of unguided surface-to-surface rockets such as the US Loral Multiple Launch Rocket System (MLRS).

Warrior Logistics
This would have a longer chassis with the rear cutaway to form a load area for the carriage of pallets of stores and ammunition with a crane being fitted for off-loading purposes.

Ambulance
This variant is the standard Warrior with the two-man turret removed and the hull modified to carry various combinations of seated and stretcher patients.

'DESERT STORM' MODIFICATIONS

All six versions of the Warrior vehicle were deployed to Saudi Arabia in the autumn of 1990 including the section vehicle, command vehicle, Mechanised Recovery Vehicle (Repair), Mechanised Combat Repair Vehicle, Mechanised Artillery Observation Vehicle and the Battery Command Vehicle, with the latter two entering service with the British Army ahead of schedule for this operation.

Most of these vehicles were sent from the British Army of the Rhine (BAOR) in Germany although some vehicles, for example the Mechanised Artillery Observation Vehicle and the Battery Command Vehicle, were sent direct from the UK. The decision to issue the Warrior MAOV to the Royal Artillery ahead of plan required training support not only from GKN, the prime contractor, but also the key sub-contractors including Dowty, GEC-Avionics and Pilkington. These vehicles were commissioned at Ludgershall in the UK and then shipped to Saudi Arabia. Before the MOAVs arrived, some of the infantry command vehicle Warriors were converted for use in the forward observation role. In

A model representation of a Warrior fitted with Trigat medium range ATGW pods. Additional missiles would be carried internally allowing the crew to reload the launchers. (GKN Defence)

addition, Warrior command vehicles were also deployed in the forward observation role for armoured regiments.

A number of the Warriors were modified for use as anti-tank vehicles fitted with the Milan ATGW. At that time the older FV432 carried the Milan teams, who dismounted from the vehicle to use the system. But the FV432 did not have the same battlefield mobility and survivability as the Warrior that it was required to protect. The order for the Warrior Milan conversion was placed with GKN Defence on 22 October 1990 and the first kits were designed, manufactured and delivered in just one week. The Milan launcher was mounted on the turret roof which enabled targets to be engaged as soon as the vehicle came to a halt, reserve missiles being carried internally. After the Gulf Conflict the British Army placed an order for additional Warriors specifically modified for this role.

To improve their battlefield survivability, all Warrior mechanised combat vehicles were fitted with additional appliqué armour once the vehicles had been deployed to the Middle East. The contract for the appliqué armour kits was placed by the MoD on 19 October 1990 and design and development, including firing trials, was completed by 4 January 1991. All of the kits were built and delivered by the start of the ground offensive on 24 February. The kit was developed by Vickers Defence Systems and is of the Chobham type, providing a high degree of protection against both chemical energy (e.g. HEAT) and kinetic energy attack.

In addition to the appliqué armour packages, many minor modifications were carried out to the Warrior, including the installation of GPS for section, infantry command and REME Warrior variants which enabled the crew to pinpoint their exact position in a matter of seconds.

Some Warriors were also modified to allow Mini Pipe Fascines to be carried in bundles along the side of the vehicle, these could be quickly removed and dropped into ditches and other battlefield obstacles to allow vehicles to cross. Incidentally, like the Challenger 1, Warriors were also fitted with maintenance free batteries for the Gulf campaign.

As the design authority, GKN Defence played a key role in ensuring that the Warrior was ready for operations in the Middle East and this was made easier due to their considerable experience with the vehicle in this part of the world. Since 1984 the Warrior had been demonstrated widely in the Middle East and a Desert Warrior was being demonstrated in a Gulf State at the time of the Iraqi invasion of Kuwait

GKN Defence not only supplied parts and modification kits for Warrior vehicles deployed to Saudi Arabia as part of Operation 'Granby'. A

Warrior undergoing vertical obstacle climbing trials in Turkey. It retains the standard British Army Vickers Defence Systems turret armed with 30mm Rarden cannon and 7.62mm MG, but has two firing ports in the rear troop compartment and an exhaust shroud. (GKN Defence)

Desert Warrior has a Delco Systems Operations two-man power operated turret armed with McDonnell Douglas Helicopters 25mm Chain Gun, 7.62mm co-axial MG, two TOW launchers, firing ports, exhaust shroud, NBC and air-conditioning system. With the TOW launchers and the 25 mm gun it has a capacity to kill enemy armoured vehicles and also fire on the move. (GKN Defence)

This warrior under evaluation by the Royal Norwegian Army has the name 'Froya' along the side of the hull. Warrior is a versatile vehicle and has proved its capabilities both in desert and Arctic conditions. The advantages of a vehicle like this particularly in extreme climates is that there is potential for protecting the crew against the elements as much as against small arms fire and air burst artillery. Artic Warrior was developed specifically to meet the requirements of the Norwegian Army and has the same turret as fitted to the Desert Warriot but without TOW launchers. (GKN Defence)

support team of GKN and other engineers was built up in Saudi Arabia and remained there until well after the ceasefire. In addition to representatives from GKN it also included staff from Perkins (powerpack) and Pilkington (optics).

NGL and Gallay were developing an air conditioning system for the Warrior and this was installed in a vehicle for some 1500km of trials, but production had not started by the time of the ground war and it was never fielded.

FUTURE DEVELOPMENTS

A Warrior mechanised combat vehicle has been used as the basis for the Vehicle Electronics Research Defence Initiative (VERDI) programme. VERDI is a joint Defence Research Agency (DRA) and UK defence industry initiative to research the benefits of the integration of modern technology into armoured fighting vehicles.

For many years computers, fire control systems and other sensors have been added to armoured fighting vehicles on an ad hoc basis, leading not only to severe integration problems but also very cluttered turrets, typified by the Chieftain/ Challenger 1 MBTs. The DRA was well aware of this problem and proposed that it and the UK defence industry should build a demonstrator to show the potential customer, the British Army, what could be achieved in a short space of time using existing sub-systems wherever possible.

In December 1988 the DRA briefed some 80 companies and by 1992 the prototype VERDI system had been completed.

The common crew stations in the hull and turret have identical computer driven data and display management for each crew member, enabling them to share or exchange roles; either crew member can call up information on their screens at the push of a button. VERDI is integrated into a standard Warrior hull and turret, but on the rear of the turret is a power operated telescopic mast on the top of which is mounted a thermal imager and image intensifier. This allows the vehicle to stay behind cover with just the mast showing. The armament of the standard Warrior is retained but a defensive aids system is fitted which allows the crew to select chaff, smoke and other obscurants according to the threat.

The Warrior turret is provided with an integrated fire control system and either the hull or turret crew member can lay the gun using thumb axis controllers. The commander has a day/thermal sight with laser rangefinder and a binocular viewer as well as having access to the images generated by the thermal imager and high resolution TV camera mounted on the mantlet, which moves in elevation with the main armament.

To enable the vehicle to find its exact position at any time GPS and an inertial navigation system (INS) is fitted. Other equipment installed on the vehicle includes a gas turbine auxiliary power unit, complete communications system and an environmental control unit and NBC system.

VERDI-2

Following the unveiling of VERDI in 1992 it was decided to move ahead with VERDI-2, again using the Warrior as a basis. VERDI-2 has a direct relevance to the British Army TRACER (Tactical Reconnaissance Armoured Combat Equipment Requirement), which aims to replace the current Scorpion CVR(T) family.

The original VERDI had a three-man crew, the driver being seated front left as normal and the two operators at the rear, one on the hull rear and one in the turret. In VERDI-2, both crew members are seated side by side in the hull towards the rear and have full access to all sensors as well as being able to drive the vehicle. Three day-TV cameras mounted on the front of the hull provide an input to the operator's screens, enabling them to drive in the fully closed down position. The crew stations of VERDI-2 are similiar to those of the first VERDI and either crewman is able to carry out the reconnaissance function.

Mounted on the hull roof is a representative turret fitted with a mockup of a medium calibre weapon system, and mounted on either side is a pod of Shorts Starstreak High Velocity Missiles (HVM). There is no facility to fire any of the weapons. Mounted on the roof will be the mast mounted sensor package fitted to the first VERDI and a Thorn EMI passive Air Defence Alert Device (ADAD).

An Alvis Stormer will be used as a troop leader's vehicle and is fitted with a VHF antenna, TV link antenna and a video camera that can be elevated and traversed. The troop leader's vehicle is able to receive and transmit information from VERDI-2 as well as with the next chain of command.

The original Vehicle Electronics Research Defence Initiative (VERDI) vehicle was based on a warrior chassis. In this photograph, taken in mid 1992, the mast mounted sight is partly raised and the turret is traversed right. (DRA/CCR)

One of the prototype Warrior chassis' fitted with the Euromissile HOT Compact Turret (HCT) with four 4000m range HOT ATGWs in the ready to launch position. The HOT combination offered potential customers an armoured vehicle which had mechanically the same parts as the APC but never entered service.

THE PLATES

Plate A: *Section vehicle, BAOR, NORTHAG, Germany, October 1990*

This section vehicle has the standard British Army green and black camouflage scheme. It carries a yellow vehicle identification number, in this case a '33' in a circle, on the hull sides and on a plate mounted on the rear of the turret bustle cage. There is a red and yellow traffic hazard sign on each of the rear stowage bins and a warning in German has been added to the right hand bin. Apart from the cam net in the turret bustle cage the vehicle is devoid of any additional external stowage.

The first unit in the British Army of the Rhine (BAOR) to receive Warrior was 1st Battalion, Grenadier Guards, who took delivery of their first vehicles in 1987 and became fully operational the following year. Until recently, all Warrior-equipped regiments were in BAOR but under 'Options for Change' there will also be two Warrior regiments based in the UK. For training purposes Warriors are also deployed to Canada at the British Army Training Unit Suffield (BATUS).

Plate B: *Section vehicle, 1st Bn., The Staffordshire Regt., southern Iraq, Operation 'Desert Sabre', 25 February 1991*

Prior to the start of the ground offensive all Warrior vehicles were fitted with applique armour packages. The only indication of this vehicle's unit is the Staffords' knot pennant flown from the radio aerial. The inverted vees on the hull sides are IFF (Indication Friend or Foe) markers adopted by the Allied units before the start of the ground war. The different geometric shapes around the vehicle numbers were generally used to indicate the parent Company. Most Warriors carried extensive additional stowage as the units were operating in the field for an extended period.

Plate C: *Section vehicle, C Coy., 1st Bn., The 22nd (Cheshire) Regt., 1 Cheshire battle group, Vitez, Bosnia, January 1993*

As part of the UK's contribution to the UN Forces operating in the former Yugoslavia, one Warrior battalion has been deployed to Bosnia. The first Warrior unit to be sent to Bosnia was 1st Battalion, The Cheshire Regiment under the command of Lt.Col. Bob Stewart. These were deployed as part of Operation Grapple along with 2nd Battalion, the Royal Irish Regiment, one squadron of 9th/12th Royal Lancers (Prince of Wales's) and 42 Field Squadron, Royal Engineers. In the early days of the deployment British vehicles often sported large Union Jack flags as additional identification. This practice was discontinued as it was felt to be incompatible with the UN's role as an International force.

Plate D: *Section vehicle, 2nd Bn., Royal Anglian Regt., Celle, Germany, March 1994*

This illustration shows the basic internal layout of the Warrior Section vehicle. Other variants such as the Command vehicle and the Artillery Observation vehicle differ quite markedly from what is shown here. The driver's cockpit is at the front left of the vehicle. The powerpack (not shown here) is positioned to the right of the cockpit and this can make the driver's position very hot. The seat is adjustable and the Warrior has a reputation for being relatively comfortable to drive. The seat can in fact be reclined completely which allows it to be used as a bed when the vehicle is halted. It also gives access to the turret and troop compartment. To the driver's left is his instrument panel and gear range selector. The panel has a speedometer, RPM indicator, fuel gauge and coolant temperature guage. In addition there are a number of warning lights and master switches. The driver also has controls for the hydraulic troop compartment door and the Halon fire extinguishers. Steering is with a simple yoke system and in front of the driver are the brake, emergency brake and accelerator. Directly behind the driver is the NBC sytem. Here the access panel is open to show the various filters. In the turret the commander's position is on the right and the gunner's on the left. Between them and immediately in front of the Rarden cannon and the Chain gun is the ready ammo storage. The radio is between the commander and gunner on the rear wall of the turret. The sliding turret cage allows access to the troop compartment behind and below the turret. There are padded benches down either side of the troop compartment and the third seat on the left hand side of the vehicle is also the chemical toilet. Immediately beyond this is the boiling vessel to heat food and prepare the compulsory 'brew'. There is stowage space for personal equipment, additional ammunition and 94mm LAW behind the seats. There is additional stowage space below some of the seats. Below the right hand bench is the piston for the power operated door and the manual control for the same. Mounted around the roof are a number of air blowers connected to the NBC and environmental control system.

Plate E1: *Mechanised Recovery Vehicle (Repair), 1st (British) Armoured Division, Operation Granby, Saudi Arabia, February 1991*

Warrior Mechanised Recovery Vehicle (Repair) has been designed to recover damaged and disabled Warrior's as well as other tracked and wheeled vehicle. This vehicle was used by 1st (British) Armoured Division during the Gulf War. Due to the harsh conditions in the Gulf it was calculated that as many as 70 per cent of vehicles might be lost to attrition and breakdowns. The success of these repair vehicles in the Gulf can be gauged by the fact that almost 100 per cent of the Warriors were operational throughout the conflict.

Plate E2: *Mechanised Combat Repair Vehicle, BAOR, NORTHAG, Germany, October 1990*

The Warrior Mechanised Combat Repair Vehicle is almost the same as the Warrior Mechanised Recovery Vehicle (Repair) except that it is not fitted with the winch or the spade at the rear. Although this means it cannot perform the recovery function of the MRV(R) its primary role is to change powerpacks and other systems in the field.

Plate F: *Maj. John Rochelle's Command Vehicle, C Company, 1st Bn., The Staffordshire Regt., Objective Lead, southern Iraq, 26 February 1991*

'Oscar Bravo' was the Company Command vehicle of C Company, 1st Battalion, The Staffords. The black vehicle callsign appears on both hull sides and on the additional stowage tins on the rear of the turret bustle cage. It also appears on the right rear stowage bin. Below this bin and on both hull sides the designation 2/3/C has been added. This was a code adopted shortly before the invasion to indicate 7th Armoured Brigade (2), 1st Battalion Staffords (3), C Company (C). 1st Staffords was involved in some of the heaviest fighting during the advance into Iraq and Kuwait, including the assaults on objectives Platinum and Lead. The Company Commander was Major John Rochelle who was awarded the Military Cross for service during the Gulf War.

Plate G: *Section vehicle, 1st Bn., 22nd (Cheshire) Regt., 1 Cheshire battle group, Zenica, Bosnia, January 1993*

This vehicle is in the standard United Nations white colour scheme and the 'UN' identification has been added on the hull front and sides and on the left rear stowage bin. It has the vehicle number '31' on the turret sides and on the right rear stowage bin which also has a black edging around all but the bottom edge. The only national identification it carries is a small Union Jack painted on the forward right side of the turret, but it has a Cheshires pennant on the right front radio aerial and flies a large UN flag from one of the rear turret aerials. The bumble bee may have been an unofficial unit marking and appeared on the right turret side just behind the smoke dischargers. The vehicle also has a Comic Relief 'squashed tomato' strategically placed on the front tow hook.

Notes sur les planches en couleur

A Ce véhicule de section porte le style de camouflage de l'Armée Britannique en vert et noir. Il porte aussi un numéro d'identification du véhicule en jaune, dans ce cas un '33' dans un cercle, sur les flancs de la caisse et sur une plaque montée à l'arrière de la cage de la tourelle. On remarque un panneau de danger à la circulation rouge et jaune sur chacun des bacs de magasinage.

B Avant le lancement de l'offensive au sol, tous les véhicules Warrior reçurent un blindage appliqué. La seule indication visible de l'unité de ce véhicule est le pennon de Stafford qui flotte sur l'antenne radio. Les V inversés sur les côtés de la caisse sont des marqueurs IFF (Indication Friend or Foe, indication ami ou ennemi) qui furent adoptés par les unités alliées peu avant le début de la guerre au sol.

C La première unité Warrior à être envoyée en Bosnie fut le 1er Bataillon du Cheshire Regiment, sous le commandement du Lt. Col. Bob Stewart. Cette unité fut déployée dans le cadre de l'Opération Grapple en même temps que le 2nd Bataillon du Royal Irish Regiment, un escadron de 9èmes/12èmes Royal Lancers (Prince of Wales) et le 42 Field Squadron, Royal Engineers.

D Cette illustration montre l'agencement interne de base du véhicule de section Warrior. Le cockpit du conducteur est à l'avant gauche du véhicule. Le siège est ajustable et le Warrior a la réputation d'être relativement confortable àconduire. A la gauche du conducteur se trouve son panneau de contrôle et le sélecteur de vitesses. La direction est prise en charge par un simple système à chape et devant le conducteur se trouvent les freins, les freins de secours et l'accélérateur. Directement derrière le conducteur se trouve le système NBC. Dans la tourelle la position du commandant est sur la droite et celle du canonnier sur la gauche. Le compartiment des troupes comporte des bancs rembourrés de chaque côté et le troisième siège à gauche du véhicule sert également de WC chimique. Immédiatement au delà se trouve l'instrument utilisé pour réchauffer de la nourriture.

E1 Le Warrior Mechanised Recovery Vehicle (Repair) a été conçu pour récupérer les Warriors endommagés et en panne ainsi que d'autres véhicules sur chaînes et sur roues. Ce véhicule fut utilisé par la 1ère Division Blindée (Britannique) durant la guerre du Golfe en février 1991. E2 Le Warrior Mechanised Combat Repair Vehicle est presque identique au Warrior Mechanised Recovery Vehicle (Repair) sauf qu'il ne comporte pas la poulie ou la bêche àl'arrière.

F 'Oscar Bravo' était le véhicule Company Command de la C Company, 1er Bataillon, The Staffords. L'emblème noir du véhicule apparaît sur les deux flancs de la caisse et sur les bacs de magasinage supplémentaires à l'arrière de la cage de la tourelle. Il apparaît également sur le bac de magasinage droit arrière. En dessous de ce bac et sur les deux flancs de la caisse la désignation 2/3/C a été ajoutée. Le commandant de la compagnie était le Major John Rochelle qui reçut la Croix Militaire pour son service durant la guerre du Golfe.

G Ce véhicule suit les couleurs standard à dominante blanche des Nations Unies. L'identification 'UN' a été ajoutée àl'avant et sur les flancs de la caisse et sur le bac de magasinage gauche arrière. Il porte le numéro de véhicule '31' sur les flancs de la tourelle et sur le bac de magasinage droit arrière qui comporte également une bordure noire tout autour à part sur sa partie inférieure. La seule identification nationale qu'il comporte est un petit Union Jack peint sur le côté droit avant de la tourelle, mais il possède un pennon des Cheshire sur l'antenne droite avant de la radio et un grand drapeau de l'ONU sur l'une des antennes de la tourelle arrière.

Farbtafeln

A Dieses Sonderfahrzeug hat das Standardtarnmuster der britischen Armee in den Farben grün und schwarz. Es ist mit einem gelben Fahrzeug-Kennzeichen, in diesem Fall die Zahl "33" in einem Kreis, auf den Rumpfseiten sowie auf einer Platte, die auf der Rückseite des Panzerturms angebracht ist, gekennzeichnet. Auf den rückwärtigen Stauräumen befindet sich jeweils ein rot und gelbes Verkehrswarnzeichen.

B Vor dem Beginn der Bodenoffensive wurden alle Warrior-Fahrzeuge mit einer applizierten Panzerung ausgerüstet. Der einzig sichtbare Hinweis auf die Einheit, der dieses Fahrzeug angehört, ist der Staffords-Knotenstander, der an der Funkantenne angebracht ist. Das umgekehrte "V"-Zeichen auf den Rumpfseiten stellt die IFF-Markierung dar (Indiz Freund oder Feind), die von den Einheiten der Alliierten kurz vor dem Start des Bodenkrieges eingeführt wurde.

C Die erste Warrior-Einheit, die nach Bosnien entsandt wurde, war das 1. Bataillon, The Cheshire Regiment, unter dem Befehlshaber Lt. Col. Bob Stewart. Diese Truppen wurden als Teil der "Operation Grapple" gemeinsam mit dem 2. Bataillon, The Royal Irish Regiment, einer Schwadron der 9./12. Royal Lancers (Prince of Wales's) und der 42. Feldschwadron, Royal Engineers eingesetzt.

D Diese Abbildung zeigt in groben Zügen das Innere des Warrior-Sonderfahrzeuges. Das Fahrerhaus befindet sich im Fahrzeug vorne links. Der Fahrersitz ist verstellbar, und der Warrior steht in dem Ruf, relativ bequem zu fahren zu sein. Zur Linken des Fahrers ist das Armaturenbrett und die Gangschaltung. Die Steuerung erfolgt mittels eines einfachen Lenkbügels. Vor dem Fahrer befindet sich die Bremse, die Notbremse und das Gaspedal. Unmittelbar hinter dem Fahrer ist das NBC-System. Im Panzerturm befindet sich die Stellung des Befehlshabers auf den rechten und die des Schützen auf der linken Seite. Auf beiden Seiten des Truppenabteils stehen gepolsterte Bänke, und der dritte Sitz auf der linken Seite des Fahrzeugs dient auch als chemische Toilette.

E1 Der motorisierte Warrior-Bergepanzer (Reparatur) dient zur Bergung beschädigter und funktionsuntüchtiger Warrior-Fahrzeuge sowie anderer Spur- und Räderfahrzeuge. Dieses Fahrzeug wurde im Februar 1991 im Golfkrieg von der 1. (britischen) Waffendivision eingesetzt. E2 Der motorisierte Warrior-Kampf-Reparaturpanzer ist mit dem motorisierten Warrior-Bergepanzer (Reparatur) fast identisch, außer daß er nicht mir der Winde und dem Schaufelsporn an der Rückseite ausgestattet ist.

F "Oscar Bravo" war das Kompanie-Kommandofahrzeug der Kompanie C, 1. Bataillon, The Staffords. Das schwarze Fahrzeug-Rufzeichen erscheint auf beiden Rumpfseiten sowie auf den zusätzlichen Stauräumen an der Rückseite des Panzerturms. Außerdem erscheint es auf dem rechten rückwärtigen Stauraum. Unterhalb dieses Stauraums und an den beiden Rumpfseiten wurde das Zeichen 2/3/C hinzugefügt. Der Befehlshaber der Kompanie war Major John Rochelle, der für den Dienst im Golfkrieg mit dem Militärkreuz ausgezeichnet wurde.

G Dieses Fahrzeug trägt die Standardfarbe der Vereinten Nationen, nämlich weiß. Das Kennzeichen der UN wurde auf der Rumpfvorderseite und den Seiten sowie auf dem rechten rückwärtigen Stauraum aufgetragen. Es trägt das Fahrzeug-Kennzeichen "31" auf den Seiten des Panzerturms und auf dem rechten rückwärtigen Stauraum, der außerdem ganz - außer am unteren Rand - schwarz eingefaßt ist. Das einzige Landeskennzeichen ist ein kleiner Union Jack auf der vorderen rechten Seite des Panzerturms, doch ist auf der vorderen vorderen Funkantenne ein Cheshires-Stander angebracht und an einer der rückwärtigen Panzerturmantennen befindet sich eine große UN-Flagge.